THE GIFT OF POETRY

Mary Wright Longstreth

A publication of

Eber & Wein Publishing

Pennsylvania

The Gift of Poetry

Library of Congress
Cataloging in Publication Data

ISBN 978-1-60880-488-7

Proudly manufactured in the United States of America by

Eber & Wein Publishing

Pennsylvania

Acknowledgements

I wish to thank my husband Lawson Longstreth Jr. for his words of encouragement over the years. In addition, I'd like to express my gratitude to my brother Russell Wright and Sally Hebbe for always believing in me.

    Some of my most inspiring poetic moments over the years occurred in the homes of my friends: Jerry and Ann Kufta, Robert and Mary Bortner, and Nancy Guthrie. Additionally, I'd like to thank friends Mary and Larry Stover, Daryl and Sue Ehrhart, Darlene Rabenstine, Dana Schult, Dayle Spitler, Helen Rice, Joanne Sullivan, Carrie Smith, and Joe and Linda O'Toole for their support. I'm so blessed to have such a wonderful group of friends.

    Above all, I want to thank my daughter Tammy and her husband Dean Heusner for all the time it took to help me edit and draft this book. Much love and thanks for being my rock throughout this poetic journey.

With love and heartfelt thanks,

Mary

Contents

Tears of Life

Here, as I look through the windows of my eyes,
I am met with quite a surprise
To confront all those memories of life comprised.

Those tears of life begin to flow like the tide.
My mind still repeats that same question: Why?
While that space so vacant remains inside.

Along with those choices, now I alone must decide.
There on the lawn, as I glance outside,
The flowers in the wind nod their heads with pride.

To hold back these tears of life I will try.
Jet streams fill the gaps above the wispy clouds way up high in the sky
While birds and geese serenade as they fly by.

Perhaps those clouds will fill with rain
Then splash away these tears of life that still remain.
With each passing day, many things change.

Yet those loving memories of you will always remain the same.
To go back to those times, there is nothing to gain.
It is the *missing you* part that causes me this sense of pain.

Let us not we dwell or complain, as an infinite number of words cannot explain
How, from these tears of life, we can come to refrain.
Still, some days, to remove these tears of life, it would take a hurricane.

Hidden Treasure

You could comb the ocean floor,
Dive to the bottom of the sea to explore,
In hopes that someday you might find a hidden treasure once more.

Watch the sky at night or gaze into the clouds so snowy white.
When the sunset slowly fades it was a beautiful sight.
These are the things that into life they bring delight.

When the days turn into weeks, so many new faces you will meet.
Some can be so unkind while others are so sweet.
If only you could find a hidden treasure it would make life complete.

There are those friendships that last forever over time.
Just knowing that she is near, brings peace of mind.
So often when the phone rings, it is your friend on the line.

Her kindness and concern goes way beyond measure.
So very rare in a lifetime will you find a friend with this behavior.
Now you see that you have found your hidden treasure.

In this friend's trust one will never wavier.
She lives so close that we could be faraway neighbors.
Having her near has done my mind a favor.

Many times this tangled web of life we together attempt to unwind.
To thank my Lord and Savior for this gift I need to take the time.
For I now have found a hidden treasure and friend combined.

Alone

Here in this room of darkness with faint shadows on the walls.
The light reflects from outside where the traffic stalls.
Now here alone with Alone I am, before daybreak calls.
Those chairs are around the table beside a desk a bit small.
Here in silence alone, many thoughts can be recalled.

To be alone yet not lonely is a depth upon life's road.
Walk through a garden of flowers and stop to smell a rose;
Through the quiet whisper one can find life's beauty exposed.
Do many find this place of wonder? How many do you suppose?
Stress does not exist here—just tranquil clear minds compose.

Come along with me on this journey together yet alone.
In this world of wandering ventures let your mind roam.
Lest not confuse a daydream with Alone in darkness known.
This light from within will lead you to a shimmer of brighter tones.
Watch this darkness filter to light when to daybreak its space does loan.

In this spinning world Alone for you will unwind.
Here the true meaning of life's wealth you will find.
So take Alone along alone to travel through your mind.
Many thoughts you will unconsciously file in categorized lines.
Open the door to happiness in your hand the key you will find.

Through the darkness alone, Alone will make your life divine.
Never fear if along the way you should stumble or fall at times.
Simplify those tears of sorrow for with smiles they will combine.
Selectively Alone chose your own path upon life's rainbow overtime.
Let Alone lead you alone into the bright sunshine.

Full Moon

I need not look up at the sky to see it on display.
For sure the full moon is not far away.
The lines of poetry easily connect in my mind today.

From the moons' lit path the words flow like an ocean wave.
This gift for me so easily finds its way.
That full moon triggers this rhyming process to engage.

The words march like soldiers as in my mind they parade.
There—feel the magnetic pull when into that full moon I gaze.
Here again my thoughts will spin into a composing phase.

Without the full moon rhyming lines become strayed.
The surrounding space feels like an enclosed cave.
In this state of mind many cherished thoughts are saved.

Challenges from past experiences the mind again replays.
Now they pass across the span of time without yesterday's delays.
Again, these renditions the full moon will prompt the mind to portray.

Ignited in connected verse for just a moment the words stay.
Quickly grasping them to print, now composed, in front of me they are displayed.
Why was that the choice of subject inscribed one might say.

In full moon the timely commands will set the scene for a play.
Never a theme planned beforehand the topic of the day.
Moonbeams of joy will shine to illuminate your path along the way.

The Daffodils

The daffodils are blooming now.
I haven't seen my sister in a while.

Three months ago she passed away.
So many things I forgot to say.

It was forever I thought she would stay.
I watched her home be sold today.

Off to that land beyond there comes the day.
He calls us home without delay.

Those daffodils she planted in the garden will stay.
Sunbeams enhance the golden petals for our Master's bouquet.

I stopped to ponder, reflect, and pray.
A woman bought her car and drove it away...

Until

Oh my, death again has come to our door.
Here we are in grief as so many times before.

This I find difficult to believe.
You have taken my sister from me.

For three years she has been ill.
She had a son; I can see her speak of him still.

She loved him with the strongest will.
She wished to live to see his dreams fulfilled.

Lord you had planned a greater thrill.
There above the highest hill.

Many tears of loss from our eyes will spill.
Over time, her loving memories this empty space will fill.

She can now rest in peace without pain, shots, or pills.
God be with her until we meet again, until…until…

Big Blue Sky

Up above the big blue sky they say that is where the angels fly.
There with those angels we too someday will soar so high.
To get used to this change we will not have to try.

The angels spread their wings and begin to sing.
Those bells will ring as to welcome the next one of us in.
Meadows so serene and green a glorious beauty it brings.

Above the big blue sky many crystal clear brooks steadily flow.
Tranquil sloping hillsides frame the spacious valleys below.
With a gentle calm the whispering winds carry a sea of fine mist so low.

Here on Earth's tabletop of life are many interchanging puzzle parts.
While others go on to begin that new distant start.
There above the big blue sky they will fly like a lark.

Leaving behind loved ones their eyes filled with tears.
Oppressed with the thought of how your time to go has appeared.
As you join with many friends their voices you will hear.

Time has a way to mend grief-stricken hearts.
For one day soon you will have made your mark.
Then leave it all behind like a masterpiece of art.

Again the angel choir will beckon the bells to chime.
Above the big blue sky they know it is now your time.
All of those materialistic things you will leave behind.

Nor those appointments will you have to make.
There you will approach Heaven's gate.
No need to stand and wait—just walk in—it is your place to take.

Life as you knew it has now passed by.
Never again will you have to worry lament or sigh.
You will now forever rest in peace above the big blue sky.

Mother

Now as I sit here with a wondering mind.
These tears their way do find.
I am remembering my mother; she was so very kind.

The illness stayed with her so very long.
Although her heart was weakening, she tried to be so strong.
If only someway, somehow my mother's life I could have prolonged.

Those birds in the trees outside her window chirped their same usual song.
It was as though they too knew something was so very wrong.
Yet I knew quite soon she would join that heavenly throng.

As so many years ago, the meaning of the word *final* I have come to know.
I miss you more than ever, Mother; although to others, I guess, it doesn't really show.
Perhaps someday I will come to define why so early in my life you had to go.

As a small child you taught me how to lead.
All things happen for a reason you taught me to believe.
There are times in your footsteps I will walk as for your comfort I still need.

Slowly this path will lead me to where together again there we will be.
Through the valleys and the sun drenched hillsides so very far I can see.
To be without you, Mother, it is still at times so very difficult for me to concede.

Although your hand I cannot reach to hold.
As I walk alone here on this road of life so bold.
Time is passing quickly as I soon will face the age of old.

Those final chapters of my life will soon begin to unfold.
I recall *I will not always be here with you*, those words to me you told.
Now all of those childhood memories I will cherish more than gold.

The seasons they will come and go bringing with them rain, sleet, and snow.
It is a mothers' love that gives this road of life its soft golden glow.
Thank you, Lord, for my mother, who, through so many years, I had come to know.

Lord, will you please remind her for me—Mother, I will forever love you so.
Now with a daughter of my own, our lives are so intertwined.
I bring to her this treasured lesson of knowledge and love combined.

In the reflection of her eyes your face I still see from time to time.
Although now I have come to find the reflection so much a resemblance of you Mother,
The face I see is really that of mine.

Over Time

Inside of me those orphaned feelings pine.
Together with an abandoned loss combine.
Could I somehow put to rest this grieving state of mind?
Then release in peace these raveling twines.
This and more will all fall into place over time.

Phrases interrupt my thoughts; as to me their way they find.
There quickly scribbled are the lines.
I am surprised in disbelief as this train of thought attempts to rewind.
Tears of grief rush forth as my plans for this day are pushed behind.
To understand this force perhaps it will embrace me over time.

Rays of bright sunshine through the windows climb.
Through the light those thoughts of you I bind.
Notions of your presence ramble through my mind like a morning glory vine.
When nighttime falls the moon so still upon this darkness shines.
This blinding path of sorrow will be cast away over time.

Loving memories follow me as I walk in faith one step at a time.
Months will turn into years as this clock of life chimes.
Like raindrops these tears of loss will be replaced with joy over time.
I am consoled by gazing at the rainbow's colorful arched lines.
Treasured written phrases will forever be the gift that you've made mine.

Reflections from the past will with today's events combine.
In Mother's footsteps I find myself walking sometimes.
Sorrowful thoughts I will need to decline.
Divine lessons learned from childhood guide me in this life of mine.
Strength woven with love will make me stronger over time.

The Stone

I placed those flowers by the stone today.
Slowly I turned to walk away.
Then as to imagine I could hear you say.

"Wait for me, isn't this a beautiful day."
Again slowly my footsteps will try to lead me away.
I pause to glance at the stone where those flowers lay.

This is where all of those unanswered questions come into play.
Are you drifting somewhere in spirit, can you see me some way?
There beneath the stone on the hillside of rocks and clay.

I again look back at the stone as I try to convince myself today
That your number was up on the day you passed away.
Now there in eternity you will always stay.

Memories of you through my mind will be forever portrayed.
Many more flowers throughout my lifetime by the stone I will lay.
Over time those flowers will wilt and perhaps drift away.

Those engraved letters on the stone are placed there for display
While once again I read your name as I pray.
To reach acceptance that you have really passed away, I may, I may…

Mary Wright Longstreth

Friend So Dear

Countless are the times spent together with a friend so dear.
Never far away is your friendship so sincere.
Memories together we made over days, weeks, months and years.
Unbroken bonds our families celebrate with holiday cheer.

Much love, joy and laughter is shared with this friend so dear.
Time stood still today as a message received became quite clear.
One's health has taken a turn that has become severe.
Our moments left to share will be few are the words I hear.

The news is that at any time your time to go could be near.
It's selfish of me to wish you could stay forever with us here.
Knowing you are gone fills my eyes with grief shedding tears.
Constant treasured reminders I will cherish of a Friend So Dear.

You

There in the house it is built of stone.
These days sometimes you may feel alone
Since your husband has gone to his heavenly home.
Your son and daughter they are both grown.
Your friends will call you on the phone.

Those words you now realize that you wanted to say.
So thankful for all of those things that you did not delay.
Although your husband has passed away,
With you those loving memories will always stay
As you recall those times from day to day.

Over the years you together watched the grandchildren play.
Now to go watch the one play soccer perhaps you may
While another one is off to college; she is on her way.
Then to visit the other one, you could go for a while to stay.
All of these things together will help to brighten your day.

Sometimes your eyes may fill with tears.
Many times you will recall memories from past years.
Time will pass quickly with friends and family near.
Life has been wonderful it is so clear.
Now as you take this stroll through life You will not fear.

Have lunch with your daughter and share stories for a spell.
She will stop by her childhood home there where you dwell.
Like her father, in the profession of education she has excelled.
With pride you think of your son; he too has done quite well.
There in the quiet stillness, another tear fell…

Memory

My mind must be on another of its forgetting sprees.
Those characteristic lines on your face have a familiarity.
Your name seems to have somehow escaped my memory.

Perhaps a friend from my childhood you could be.
It looks like some resemblance there to that I do agree.
Many different smiles pass through my memory then leave.

The usual time of recall it already did exceed.
Several different names are going through my mind at lightning speed.
The name I am searching for is not any of the ones I see.

Amazingly the name I need just went through my memory.
I caught a glimpse of it as it passed by me.
For a moment I must pause to get a grip on this reality.

Maybe it will retrace that channel in my memory.
A blank space so often intercedes.
I will soon put a name to that face I do believe.

If I could acknowledge that I forgot, my mind would be relieved.
There might be some frayed assembly in my memory.
Hopefully the dots will connect and then the name is weaved.

There must be some way for me to recall your identity.
Had I met you near the ocean or was it by the sea.
I think there is a vitamin that can restore this loss of memory.

This plight is becoming exhausting for me.
I'll take a break from this and make a cup of tea.
With each sip I will forget how difficult remembering names can be.

There's the name I need; it just came back to me.
Now if I could recall that face from this situation I would be freed.
Maybe what's-her-name could help me fix my mixed-up memory.

Alphabet of Tribute

Those new faces we met and the many friendships made at the start of school for a lifetime they will last.
As you recall, to learn the alphabet was one of our first tasks.
A is for Apple
B is for Ball
C is for Cat
D is for Dog
This seemed to be so very basic to all of us back there in the past.
Now we gather here again with members of our class.
Forty years has gone by so very fast.

While reading the hometown newspaper I notice that another of our classmates passed away.
That makes number twelve as the rest of us for now together here we will stay.
The first loss was Rochelle Myers; our sadness is beyond what any words or grief could convey.
Life changes many things along the way.
Now with the alphabet, let's begin again with the letter A.
Recently the number has changed to thirteen that has passed away.

A is for Adams, A is for Alvin, A is for all
B is for Behr, B is for Bertha, B is for Biddle, B is for Bitting
C is for Chism
D is for Davis, D is for Dick, D is for Dudley
E is for Elizabeth, E is for ending
F is for Fleisher, F is for Finton
G is for gone
H is for Heaven
I is for imagine
J is for James, J is for Jonas, J is for Joyce
K is for Kretzing
L is for Laverne, L is for Liz, L is for last
M is for Myers, M is for memories
N is for now
O is for over
P is for people, P is for places
Q is for questions
R is for Rochelle, R is for rest
S is for Saundra, S is for Strunk
T is for Tom, T is for together
U is for us

V is for victories
W is for Walter, W is for Waync, W is for we, W is for will
X is for which one of us will be next
Y is for you, Y is for years
Z is for zero

Now you see the many faces, places with the victories we together won. Names, questions, and many memories will last over the years, when the last one of us has gone to rest in Heaven, ending us all. Imagine! Imagine!

Marbles

Imagine for twelve years marbles being placed in a jar side by side.
Upon graduation day the marbles scattered as the jar is opened wide.
The time has come to explore the vast world outside.

Taking with us the wisdom and knowledge acquired at the great Newport High,
We marbles each chose our destiny with pride.
What number of years to reunite? We decided five.

With whatever turns of life's events before us, we strived to survive.
One of the marbles rolled so far it got lost at sea in the ocean tide.
Twenty-one others over the years were sent to heaven to reside.

Like round marbles through life's misfortunes and triumphs we glide.
Alas, the meaning of the golden years we have suddenly come to realize.
For fifty years we tried to look older, but now buy lotions and potions our age to defy.

Meeting together in our hometown to each other we are forever tied.
Tonight we extend our heartfelt thanks to the teachers, for our lives they did guide.
Through this maze of life, the lesson of how to roll as marbles could be applied.

This dynamic journey of making memories is quite a ride.
To share our remembrances, a few marbles are prescribed.
Hold these marbles in your hand, laugh, and smile; wipe away any tears you cried.

Let's see how many of us still have all our marbles when the next reunion arrives?
We will take joy and happiness as we journey onward, our Class of 1965.
We might hear someone say, "I forgot my marbles oh my, oh my…"

Before Dark

There is a cookie in the cookie jar.
A penny in the sugar bowl
Save the sparks in the fireplace to start.
I'm leaving,
But will return to you some evening,
Someday soon before dark.

Do not start to doubt me
As you sit and wonder where I will be.
When you look at the maple tree
The leaves are blowing oh so free,
But the roots are planted firmly in the ground;
My love for you will always be around.

When you reach for the cookie jar
You know that I am not so far.
I just wished upon a star;
It is shining where you are.
While bright moonbeams connect our hearts
Now you know I will return before dark.

The Power Line

I was just a little girl, not past five years old,
When a big truck came rumbling down our lane.
This is the story the driver told.
The power line is going across your farm, but it cannot do any harm.

Then Dad replied in great alarm,
What will become of the farm!
How can I make a sweet potato bed
With all of those wires strung over my head?

It was agreed they could go across if they paid a fee.
Then my brothers got as busy as the bees.
When the trees were cut they burned the brush.
They were paid to watch the fires from dusk till dawn till dusk.

The brothers—they were just young boys—
Spent their pay on howdy dowdy toys.
The linemen placed the towers still
Way up on the top of the highest hills.

As I grew older I still recall those three towers straight and tall.
If ever you have a wondering mind,
You will remember the hay-making times
Out underneath the power line.

Bullfrog Hollow

If you want a place to meditate
Where no one else can concentrate,
Go to bullfrog hollow in the evening.
Because if you are country folk
You will never get provoked.
When you hear the bullfrogs croak in the hollow.

It's a cool quiet place where the bullfrogs debate.
Although it isn't late, you would never ever wait
For the bullfrogs to hesitate, while you took time to meditate.
The bullfrogs sat on the rocks with the moss carpet for their feet,
On the banks of the cool narrow stream
That flows through bullfrog hollow.

It was there we had a playhouse my sisters and me.
We would swing on the grapevine that hung from a tall oak tree.
That cup of sassafras tea, we sweetened with teaberries.
Those days will always stay in my Bullfrog Hollow memories.
Two sisters and six brothers in Heaven perhaps bullfrogs they can see.
Together with our father and mother, they wait for my brother and me.

When folks would visit our home in the evening
They would sit on the steps of the back porch
And talk about the price of wheat, politics, and scarcity of horseshoe nails.
Then all of a sudden someone would say,
Listen to the bullfrogs down the way.
The most refreshing sound to hear in the county.

No one will ever know real country life
Till they spend an evening on the banks of the narrow stream
That has a moss carpet for your feet and a grapevine for your seat
While you listen to the beat of the bullfrogs strong repeat.
There is not a better place to meditate in these United States.
How I long for that old home place of bullfrog hollow in the evening.

Charm Bracelet

Today after a long conversation I hung up the phone.
I was reminiscing with a friend, since high school I have known.
She spoke of a charm bracelet she used to own.
It got misplaced when she moved into another home.
The loss of it, in her voice carried a sad tone.
I recall when she wore it on her wrist, how brightly it had shone.

Today this task I can no longer postpone.
I packed a new charm bracelet into a box for her to own.
Off I go, to mail it to that friend, for so many years I have known.
Those charms will serve as cherished mementos.
On the links of the silver chain they will hang all alone.

Years ago, she moved away from Frog Hollow Road where the strawberries were grown.
Recalling many memories of loss and grief, how quickly time has flown.
Our everlasting friendship we still maintain over the phone.
This new charm bracelet will not replace the old one she used to own.
Someday she will smile as she recalls the day this gift was delivered to her home.
It was sent to her with love from that friend, since high school she has known.

My Little Buffalo Fish Poem

Nearly forty years have gone by since I rode the school bus that traveled from the ridge, then turned down to the road below and then crossed over the Little Buffalo. The bus would follow the road around and then we would arrive in town, where we attended school. At the end of the day, back up through the Little Buffalo the bus would go. After graduation I moved away. My sister called me one day to say, "They are taking the covered bridge away! They are moving it and changing things around to build a state park. Folks will come from everywhere to fish here from dawn to dark!"

It was not very long after that day that I got another call. This time I heard her say, "They are going to start! The covered bridge they moved downstream." This all sounded like what might have been a dream.

Time has gone by; the years have passed. One day I took my fishing rod, tackle box, and bait and off I went. I cast my line there by the water's edge of the Little Buffalo. I would wait. The folks fishing upstream were visiting from another state. Each time that they cast a line, it seemed another fish they would take.

This will not take long as I'll have my limit at least by noon I thought. I remembered all of the basic skills of how to catch a fish I was taught as a small child. I packed my lunch and took it along with me; I packed a lot.

It was not long until I realized these fish here; they can relate! They would just swim around as if to say, "You are a familiar face we know. You moved away from this area some time ago. You see we do not want to go. We fish like these cool, clear waters here in the Little Buffalo. Just throw us a line with lots of bait to let us know that you, like many others who have moved away, just came back home to spend the day."

The fish knew I understood, and to come back here to fish many times again, I would!

As the fish begin to age over time, their scales grow thin; they could be going blind. It will be a day around that time there I will find the largest fish of its kind. I will take that fish I fed all that bait! Oh, it sure will have been worth the wait. I will have it mounted on a plaque and hang it on my wall. Then when I too grow old and can barely see within my heart those memories will be. It is then that I will recall, there is this place in winter, spring, summer, and fall. It is the greatest place of all to go. There along water's edge of the Little Buffalo. So take some time to cast a line, or just spend a day here to unwind. You too then will agree with me that this certainly is a place of heavenly tranquility. Over time many changes you will come to know, but the water will always steadily flow, there by the bridge of the Little Buffalo.

The Old Covered Bridge

The old covered bridge on the Buffalo Creek
Was moved downstream back last week
When Uncle Sam said that it has to go
For Project 70 we all know.
It is a great big dam and a state park—
Somewhere for us to go from dawn 'til dark

The homesteads were sold to the government,
When folks who lived there gave their consent
For Project 70's residence.
It is situated on the fields where they used to dwell,
Before the time had come for them to sell.

If the old covered bridge only had a mind,
To tell the stories left behind,
But only the homefolks who lived there know
Of the happiness they shared before they had to go
Along with the old covered bridge of the Little Buffalo.

The times they will spend at the state park,
Will never replace the memories in their hearts,
Of the cattle, the turkeys, and the collie dogs' bark,
While the old covered bridge now stands alone,
At the Little Buffalo State Park.

Walk

If you walk through this world in darkness, there your life will hide.
Then not see the joys beyond the blinders you placed before your eyes.
Cast away those holding bars that cage your mind inside.

Walk tall upon the earthen sod—there you will see this world so wide.
Find someone to share your life with as you walk side by side.
Many decisions in life one by one you will together comprise.

Walk forward as you allow your face to fill with sunshine.
Gaze your eyes upon the wonders that through the landscape entwine.
Watch the raindrops soothe the flower petals as to awaken springtime.

Those many childhood memories you will replay in your mind.
Let today's lasting memory become tomorrow's quiet times.
Cultivate your finds in life as those things lost remain behind.

Tomorrow is now just a glimmer of brightness.
Yesterday is but a shadow of compressed forgotten guess.
Today walk on solid steps as you put Life's wisdom to the test.

All of this may seem frivolous to you now.
Through these lines walk your way to happiness when time allows.
Stand before a tall wide mirror and to yourself give a proud deserving bow.

On this path your footsteps will linger when your time here has declined.
As into the sunset you walk this reassurance there you will find.
From the start, I have all along been tightly holding your hand in mine.

Unseen Tears

Is that right is the frequent response one does often hear.
Never for the subject does the connection seem clear.
Seen by many much collected nothing is scattered from there to here.
Overshadowed with kindness, smiling, those eyes of interest appears.

Underneath the shade there awaits so many unseen tears.
Once removed this veil of strength is like an apple newly peeled.
Hidden in the stitch of threads dried are those unseen tears.
Memories of relented times once intact have now disappeared.

Unknown ahead this lucid space now into the windows peer.
Gone are those bright illusions for so long revered,
While storms of destruction by high winds are steered.
It seems nothing can break that barrier of those unseen tears.

For awaits an explanation to those who cannot cohere.
Underneath the surface to so few are visible those unseen tears.
Endless hours of unappreciated efforts seem placed over many years.
Quickly walk beyond the yesterdays, for tomorrow will bring cheer.

Those unseen tears have now created this sparkling river crystal clear.
From there it ripples along the winding path of life so near.
Vibrant rainbows wait to fill the seats vacated by those unseen tears.
The threaded needle mends raveled edges as it competes with time to heal.

Fear

Perhaps one has become a bit confused.
There appears to be a display of fear one might conclude.
This constriction needs swiftly to be refused.

Surely that thought can be removed.
Have all of those judgments come from you?
This being a description of someone you once knew.

Sometimes the mind can function so clear.
While one's life is glowing in those prime years.
Will this stability endure or out of fear will it spin into a broken seal.

So many of those memories you hold close to your heart so dear.
Shall empty moments these erase when you feel consumed by fear?
Could those yesterdays let go as they no longer in your hands adhere.

The days seem shorter as time appears to have shifted gears.
Thus those latter journeys of life are quickly approaching near,
As lightning's illuminating flashes grasp shining moments without fear.

The birds' chirps now silenced along with voice but a whisper mere.
One's mind a land now resurrected from past remembrances concealed.
The elder years lavish fear of change as with a slower pace they deal.

Accumulations of knowledge wasted in fear as into the empty space it stares.
Now to sit alone in question of will anyone again take time to care.
My feeble mind shall not surrender to lingering fear for it I am aware.

Many thoughts seem to get off track inside this mind so frail.
Fear maneuvers in fast pace as here it is repeatedly through faith derailed.
Without fear I will follow this road alone to those golden stairs.

The Leak

There at an office where I am employed to clean,
On the floor of the men's room was a large stream.
It was quite deep and wide it did seem.
This place employs roofers who walk above beams.

Yet there from above the water does drop—
Not sure from where the exact spot.
I wiped it all dry with my trusty string mop
In hopes that before long the leak it does stop.

Wait until tomorrow on your way to the shop.
If you spy a roofer on jet skis do not stop.
He could be wearing goulashes that lock.
You then can rest assured that the leak still drops.

So if you arrive at work today
And there on your desk this poem does lay,
Then you will know it did not float away.
Perhaps by now a plumber is on the way.

As those roofers arrived at work, the leak they did explore.
The water had consumed the entire floor.
It was so deep they could barely speak.
The hammers and nails were totally out of reach.

In their minds they too question what caused the leak.
This unsolved mystery is kind of neat.
What do we say when with the boss we meet?
Why does the roofing company's floor look like a creek?

Medical Treason

I went to the medical place for a check-up today.
It was quite surprising as to what they had to say:
Now my blood pressure it is okay.
They say my heart is beating in a slow sort of way.
Perhaps I should just go home for the rest of the day.

From that place to another medical place I had to go.
So off I went to see what the ECO had to show.
On my way I met a friend; how am I feeling, she wanted to know.
I explained to her I feel fine, but my heartbeat is slow.
I guess to her too this came as somewhat of a blow.

To come with me out of concern, she did kind of plea.
I reassured her there was not any need.
I really did feel quite well indeed.
From this medical treason I set myself free.
The time on my watch seemed to be picking up speed.

The doctor asked if I am stressed.
So stress they will consider next.
Perhaps it is the doctor's far-out guess.
He is to be one the best.
This felt like a medical treason contest.

The stress word is the one that I question.
Why would they have made such a suggestion?
Could they be headed in the wrong direction?
Shouldn't it be my heart that needs checking?
The answers to all of the questions I am not detecting.

It is now time for me to put on my coat.
On a card another appointment they wrote.
There really is nothing wrong with me, I hope.
There is a small café; a cup of tea is what I needed the most.
It would be so soothing to my throat.

I was shocked that I was still breathing.
I called a friend on the phone that evening.
I told her my prognosis was not very pleasing.
She told me all things happen for a reason.
Could all of this be some sort of medical treason?

Perhaps to this medical place I will return.
To find from the last test what results learned.
For now, with none of that is my mind concerned.
From those thoughts of today I need to myself adjourn.
For a long vacation to anywhere I now do yearn.

My heart seems to feel fine; it is still beating.
The flight reservations I am completing.
On the next plane I am leaving.
Many new adventurous places I will be seeing.
From this medical treason I will to be fleeing.

The plane is gaining altitude.
There is only one person on this plane that I knew.
We now have climbed up high into the big wide blue.
Thoughts of this medical situation in my mind are renewed.
There isn't anything about it up here that I can do.

I am way too far above the ground.
If only I could step outside to take a look around.
At that medical place these thoughts would be compound.
I will remain in this seat with a lot of strangers all around.
Many have a cough; it could be contagious as bad as it sounds.

Now I have started sneezing; I am becoming a bit concerned.
If by chance from this flight I should not return.
There may be a lesson in this medical treason to learn.
Whatever my condition I might try to get a diagnosis confirmed.
In a funny sort of way this task of a vacation I feel I have earned.

Picture on the Mantel

Today I walked into the room.
Upon the mantel it was displayed.
That picture on the mantel was placed in a very special way.
It had matting around for it in place to stay.

It was a picture of a wooden chair.
Into a black frame it had been placed with care.
Did it perhaps belong to a set somewhere?
To any other picture this cannot be compared.

That chair in the picture on the mantel it is all alone.
To whom it belonged to me it is unknown.
Perhaps many years ago that chair did grace a home.
There upon the mantel its beauty shone.

Was it one of a kind like no other?
Could it have belonged to a mother?
There placed into that frame for me to discover.
Is the picture on the mantel in remembrance of a lost lover?

Yet at that picture a second glance I take.
My mind wonders why this has in this special spot been placed.
The chair is now empty as though it will wait.
Could it hold those many memories that time cannot erase?

Was it once occupied by someone as they watched the falling rain?
In the evening maybe it served as a resting place from the day's refrain.
From where had that chair originally come?
Should I ask if to me this could be explained?

To find the reason why this picture was framed nothing would be gained.
With much uncertainty this mystery will with me remain.
That unspoken beauty in the picture on the mantel will always be the same.
There it will rest for now inside that black wooden frame.

Traveling

Through one's mind this forever changing journey of life goes traveling for a time.
Not always traveling forward, it will stop at places often left behind.
Those memories are ignited by a fallen snow or perhaps the early morning sunshine.

Traveling often on those lanes where shellbark trees grew in a line,
The traveling train is a welcome sight on the seldom used track part of a main line.
From the sweet shrub bush a start was taken along to plant at the new digs of mine.

Feathers lost from peacocks traveling strut across the lawn was a nice collected find.
The hanging lamps soft light went traveling above the table where we dined.
It was fun relaxing in that house for tea, brunch, snacks, or a glass of wine.

Family, a dog, Jazz the cat and class reunions are traveling in this memory rewind.
Some adventures were Africa, Greece, Antarctica and traveling down the Rhine.
The tray birdfeeder stood in the garden among many varieties of flowers combined.

Traveling mentally to the here and now that notion of slowing down is declined.
Grasping steadfast spiritually my Father will grant many more trails of traveling divine.
Mother's antique furniture and a new piano was put in this home without stairs to climb.

Traveling through life is like needles rejuvenating on a tree of pine.
Here printed out of words these phrases are sealed into rhymes.
This treasured recollection of me was sent from a poetic friend so very kind.

Church Bazaar

We stopped at a church bazaar today.
Inside the door was a newly published book placed on display.
The book I purchased as with this author and I did chat away.

Then across the room I made my way.
There I spied a homemade quilt of appliqué.
The Noah's ark clock, teapot, and Old World Santa were among the array.

This bazaar certainly was a warm friendly place.
Many tables were filled with sweets these ladies had baked.
Now this leaves me with many choices to make.

This church seems to have quite a large congregation.
It appears to have members with much dedication.
Each one fills their task of participation.

The church cookbook, titled *A Taste of Heaven* is for sale.
This with the approaching holiday season I can use without fail.
Then prepare many goodies to decorate in festive detail.

In this church kitchen many working angels you will find.
The food they have prepared tastes so divine.
Candles of wood and unique things make this church bazaar one of a kind.

On the front lawn of this church they placed a church bazaar sign.
Inside upon God's blueprint each member represents a scaled line.
While there His silent echoes become etched into your mind.

Stop at a church bazaar, go inside, and slow down time.
See how these working-in-numbers equations are combined.
While there in this house of faith God's love intertwines.

Bazaar Chain That Never Broke

Just a few years ago the poem "Church Bazaar" I wrote.
Today is the bazaar on my calendar I made a note
It is chilly out so to get there I will need to wear a coat.

There I saw an afghan, throws, pictures in frames, and a birdhouse on a post.
The Tea for 8 would be fun to host.
The Tiffany lamp I liked the most.

The bear wearing railroad attire will be found under someone's Christmas tree I hope.
I put Aunt Pat's handmade shepherds into my tote.
Gingerbread cakes decorated with candy corn faces were made by some creative folk.

Together the smell of soup and burgers for a sale there is not a need to coax.
No other bazaar for organization by comparison can come close.
Come pull up a chair this certainly is a swell place to loaf.

Those homemade greeting cards had a tea bag pouch.
The gooseberry jam I bought as a joke.
The jam on the table beside my Thanksgiving bird for turkey cruelty it did boast!

On that first bite of Tom's drumstick I did choke.
Lord can you please forgive me as I forgot you also blessed the roast.
I learned my lesson that turkey's temper had been provoked.

Perhaps the rest of the gooseberry jam I should compost.
Next year surrounded on a platter of herbs my holiday foul will soak.
Then it will not be tormented by some jelly hoax.

That church bazaar is the very best mentally I cast my vote.
Until the next time God will embrace all of you in his cloak.
Those angels have once again added more links to the bazaar chain that never broke.

Grandma

There is a shower forecast for today.
Place those umbrellas all away.
That is what I heard the soon-to-be-grandma say.

This will be the first grandchild for this family to arrive.
Oh how Grandma will beam with pride.
For the new parents what a blessing this new child will provide.

Let's celebrate it is time to have a cup of tea.
The joy this new child will bring, along with teddy bears and toys we will see.
In Grandma's house do you foresee a nursery?

Will this child ride on a bus, train, or horseback when it commutes.
Wait there is another route.
Grandpa reserved a seat at the airport they will group.

Way up high in the sky
In his plane they can fly.
Is that a tear in Grandma's eye?

The great-grandparents are also here to send cheer your way.
One great-grandmother passed away eleven months ago today.
Through the heavenly winds whisper her unending love and memory will stay.

As we wait from day to day until this new child arrives to stay.
We then will hear this new grandma say what a lovely splendid day.
This shower will be a stepping stone along the new grandchild's life's way.

Snowbaby

Usually the holiday season brings with it much anticipation.
Those trees glistening with snow crystals demand our concentration.
Let's put those thoughts aside as we focus on this celebration.
This young couple has in mind a greater expectation.

Today I saw snowbabies placed on the tabletop in formation.
Clearly a snowbaby will dominate today's conversation.
The guests have all arrived at this shower of elation.
This will certainly be a wonderful day of relaxation.

Today at the home of the grandparents-to-be the guests did meet.
Outside those stately oak trees in autumn flair will take a back seat.
For attention with this snowbaby shower they will need to compete.
The arrival of this child will make this holiday season complete.

On the way to New York will Grandpa pass Santa during the flight?
By the time this snowbaby arrives will the sleigh be totally out of sight?
Will New Year's be the baby's arrival date perhaps it might?
Whatever the day, it will bring grandma much joy and delight.

These new parents may learn to sleep in rotation.
Let us watch as this snowbaby melts the parents' hearts without hesitation.
This household of two will soon become three with much admiration.
This snowbaby will make its mark upon this generation.

Perhaps for a while some days will turn into nights.
This snowbaby may teach new lessons on how excitement to ignite.
While these highly skilled parents to each other hold on tight.
This shower will pave the way to this child's glowing path of life.

Confusion

When it comes to confusion I could easily pass this test.
Before now with decision making I could shine with all of the rest.
There standing tall I would mingle with the best.

Now it appears with knowledge I seem to comprehend so much less.
Those TV remotes with so many buttons really are a mess.
Today I barely conquered the task at my closet of choosing a dress.

After all of that confusion I really do need to take a rest.
Things are changing and moving fast I don't want to sound like a pest.
So much love and joy surrounds me yet I am enjoying it less.

Willful motions and repeated words, well that notion is only jest.
Today mistaking orange juice for cream in my morning coffee added zest.
Arrangements are in the making for me to leave behind my cozy nest.

That autumn chill makes me want to wear a colored leaf decorated vest.
At this point of confusion I do not need to catch a cold on my chest.
Considering all of life's disruptions I really have been blessed.

On my clear thinking days I ponder what next will they suggest.
We agreed on a place for me to go the plans are all set.
To deals with all of those unknown faces I just am not ready for that yet.

Now this decision making will soon become a toss-up of bets.
I will enjoy this ride while mumbling as I tell myself oftentimes to just say yes.
Through all of this confusion I really should be grateful I guess, I guess…

Journey's End

My dear friends' mother has taken another turn on her journey's end.
Childhood memories flash back to her as she rounds the bend.
Her path ahead is only a guess to us from the few messages she sends.

Her own mother has come to guide her on this journey's end.
This guardian angel is with her now on God we can depend.
Comfort wrapped in compassion is all that is left for us to extend.

Knowing this joy and love in our hearts we have on lend.
Borrowed time here overshadowed cannot compare to her waiting journey's end.
Time-filled days of letting go while waiting have begun to blend.

Although her earthly time has passed someday we will be joined together again.
She has left behind glorious blessings of grace and kindness for my dear friend.
Shining doors of new beginnings open as her grieving sorrow and loss will mend.

Never wavering with steadfast courage and strength to your duties you did attend.
Say goodbye to vibrant autumn leaves, passing time, and the question of when.
Today this splendid life has reached its destination to its journey's end.

To her son, daughter, and in-laws this legacy of family love she extends.
Tears of loss will be dried as this new day for the grandchildren begins.
Cherished everlasting memories to treasure she leaves for my dear friend.

Snow Ball

To attend this snow ball we will need to take a brisk hike.
Let's mingle with the evergreens in their gowns of white.
Waltzing in the winters' gale is a beautiful sight.

Those royal star magnolia buds sparkle covered with ice.
The hillsides are tucked beneath their blankets just right.
Many maple branches are bending low and snap they just might.

Holly with shining red berries stands tall throughout this bitter cold night.
Dancing at this snow ball certainly is a delight.
Snowmen dot the landscape wearing top hats, coal faces, and smiles clenching a pipe.

The cypress hedge sways in the moonlight.
To save these lavish decorations by daybreak with the warm sun it will be a fight.
The sycamores spotted dresses are camouflaged with patches attached real tight.

Flaky snacks are being served each one a refreshing cold bite.
The rock garden edges looks like flowing fountains as the closing clock strikes.
Let's not leave the snow ball until those wild geese take off in flight.

The Meadow

Go up over the hill outside of town.
On the right side of the road you will notice the fairgrounds.
As you travel farther through the valley and down,
You will see a covered bridge it is painted red all around.
It is across the big buffalo creek where lots of trees abound.

Turn left at the meadow as you drive in around.
There on this day many familiar faces can be found.
Once a year relatives reunite at the pavilion they all surround.
The small white lovely cottage has a path leading down.
Footsteps of past generations are embedded in the ground.

Up on the porch chairs are placed to lounge.
The horseshoe pitch at the meadow makes a clinking sound.
The large buffet on the table is a colorful array of mounds.
In the traditional cake walk we all go around and around.
Those passed-away loved ones are with us in silent profound.

Some years we watched the raindrops through the trees pound.
We took a family reunion picture as past memories resound.
We all gather in hopes that next year's numbers will compound.
Our footprints are among the moss and teaberry plants on the ground.
This year another chapter of us all at the meadow will be bound.

Squirrels' Lament

That bird feeder hangs centered on the long wire so free.
This squirrels' lament, it is impossible for me to reach as you can see.
My nest is built way up near the top of this white oak tree.

One would assume, me being a squirrel, I have high self-esteem.
To reach that feeder I need to become an expert on a fine wire trapeze.
From this view of the world a squirrels' lament becomes weaved.

Those feathered friends fly onto the feeder pegs to dine on gourmet seeds.
Here I hang on the front lines of a firing squad's company.
This squirrels' lament—is there any way for me to escape this misery?

Long are the days as I watch the woodpecker search for grubs, bugs, and bees.
It pecks potholes in this tree bark as a squirrels' lament destruction I do not need.
As I scurry along this horizontal path my wish is for that woodpecker to flee.

If my fur coat feathers it could be this squirrels' lament is now a dream.
Perhaps I could dress up like an owl on Halloween.
Those folks inside will slide open the door and peer through the screen.

They will get on their knees and begin to laugh, howl, and scream.
A squirrels' lament is to perch at that birdfeeder and look real keen.
They are taking pictures of me in my feathered costume; I am on the bird's team.

Back to my nest I will retreat; there against a pillow of leaves I will lean.
Many days a squirrel must think of wild schemes.
To go to the bird feeder tomorrow, the consequence could be extreme.

From my adventures at that bird feeder over time much knowledge I have achieved.
I must get healthy on acorns before I plan another bird feeder snack shopping spree.
The bird feeder could cause my demise, and the family inside agrees.

Changing Seasons

Those flowers of summer are fading fast.
The butterflies parade across the blooms making a bright contrast.
Many days of soaring temperatures have ended at last.

Trees filled with leaves display many shades of the color green.
They are about to present their autumn scene
Then frame the harvest fields that have just been gleaned.

All of this to us brings the changing seasons.
To many this change is quite pleasing,
While to those with allergies it causes a lot of sneezing.

Its beauty is beyond compare.
Those vibrant colored leaves are now everywhere.
To complain we do not dare.

Many pumpkins we have placed outside to decorate with care.
It is time to attend the county fair.
I need to find some sweaters to wear.

The yellow finch's color has begun to change.
They hang onto the heads of the sunflowers they have claimed.
Throughout the changing seasons they will remain.

I caught myself talking to the scarecrows.
Three of them I have placed in the garden row.
These changing seasons can cause your mind for a moment to go.

Up the street on the lawn, I saw some ghosts.
They danced and turned their heads; could that have been a joke?
This season I seem to enjoy the most.

For a while, time we could stop to watch
From our rocking chairs and see squirrels carry food to the treetops.
The rabbits hop across the lawn as the leaves begin to drop.

That all in a dreamer's mind would be so neat.
The changing seasons cycle must quickly complete.
With those howling winter winds it will soon need to compete.

Each day of life we must take in stride.
Let those joys of nature through your mind take a ride.
Then travel with the changing seasons as your tour guide.

Newspaper Columns

For many years upon the shelf my folk's notebooks have stayed.
They are filled with weekly newspaper columns from yesterday.
Our parents wrote about their friends and neighbors life ways.

On a farm, one son and two daughters were raised.
For the three of us children many fond memories had been made.
Their lives long past but those newspaper columns I saved.

Before me on the tabletop these newspaper columns I laid.
In disbelief at this treasure trove, our legacy I gaze.
While leafing through the many pages it seems like a maze.

Back then, writing local newspaper columns was quite the rage.
Never from roots of kindness can words written in love be frayed.
We still reminisce of the joys and happiness of those days.

From the slow-paced lifestyle we appear to have strayed.
Now news is being propelled by this new computer age.
These days newspaper columns are instantly relayed.

Forever cherished, this keepsake collection I would never trade.
Perhaps these newspaper columns could be republished someday.
If only once again our parents could stand before us to smile and wave.

Long Ago

Have you taken the time to reminisce of an acquaintance from long ago?
Today I recall memories of that petite grand lady I had come to know.
She lived in this home for over fifty years before to a retirement village she chose to go.

For two years a couple resided here and then in the wind a For Sale sign did blow.
That is when I bought this home ten years ago and met the lady who lived here long ago.
She told me the home had a long porch and two front doors; her scrapbook photo did show.

Along the garage a postage stamp shaped flower garden she planted long ago.
Bricks that came from a York trolley track she neatly placed in a row.
There is a fireplace also made of those bricks near the pear tree below.

Those pink hyacinths add a brilliant luster with their vibrant glow.
Could she be sending springtime sediments of fond memories from long ago?
Now they bring those joys to me that she had come to know.

Many pies were baked from that mound of rhubarb she used to fertilize and hoe.
The hedge of barberry and the old black iron fence surrounds the lawn from long ago.
In the old gardens the yellow finch perch on the sunflower heads hanging low.

The children's initials are painted on the basement wall; their age cannot be slowed.
With happy tears she wished for me to grace this home with pride as she did long ago.
Such a short time I had to spend with her before that land beyond her life now bestows.

This home built in 1825 of logs now covered with bricks was molded with love long ago.
Out in front, the two-hundred-year-old sycamore tree's time has come to go.
Progress can change a landscape, but overshadowed seeds of memories will always grow.

Celebration Sweet Sixteen

Mother planned this celebration sweet sixteen party for me.
This is a surprise and I am really special as you can see.
Here at this tea room we are sipping tea.

Except for my boyfriend this invite is "Ladies Only Please."
It is exciting sharing this happy time with my friends and family.
Celebration sweet sixteen has me guessing what my gifts will be.

Money to buy a car is one gift that I really do need.
Anxiously awaiting to drive; the highway signs I must heed.
This week will pass by at lightning speed; yikes, did I say speed?

Going fishing and horseback riding for my life adds glee.
Thanks, Mom, for my party filled with love and hugs as we leave.
This celebration sweet sixteen takes the cake we all agree.

Flower Girl

Her long flouncing dress was white.
It has an orange sash and a large bow tied tight.
The curls in her hair are styled with a flair just right.

This darling flower girl arrived at the reception early tonight.
She danced and danced on the floor—such a delight.
To join her to dance many little friends she did invite.

Dancing in rhythmic step she sure is a charming sight.
Never showing signs of tiring for sleep there is not a fight.
This star quality flower girl—to dance on a large stage someday she might.

Before the arrival of the bride and groom she stole the show alright.
When the wedding cake is served will she make time to take a bite?
Two large lavish wreaths on the wall added sparkle to the night.

While honeymooning in Las Vegas this couple can watch folks roll the dice.
I'll bet to ask the flower girl for a repeat performance—no need to ask twice.
She dances in her bare feet as though she is gliding over ice.

Great-grandma and the grandparents to their lives this flower girl adds spice.
For this precious flower girl to have a photo album of this day would be so nice.
Her dancing performance is now a priceless wedding gift to Daddy and his wife.

The Train

Today I am going on a destination that to me the surroundings are unknown.
The train with me aboard pulled away from the station not far from my home.
Many conversations I have had for weeks with a person over the phone.

Here traveling to get acquainted face to face I am all alone.
This is a new experience for me in the wide world with space to loan.
Until now time was a holding fence, but I have this need to roam.

Upon this new path of life ahead of me I will follow each stepping stone.
Much happiness and joy is wished for me from friends and family back home.
Across the flats I can see the sun rise and set, as the sound of the train sets the tone.

With much anticipation this trip I could no longer postpone.
There are many new adventures to endure along with a different time zone.
On the train with misty eyes and lots of pride, this journey I will take on my own.

Locomotive

The locomotive pulls away from the station with another one to it attached.
Up ahead waiting to be explored lies a new set of tracks.
Traveling at high speed the locomotive's notion is not that of looking back.

Going through the valleys, across bridges, up steep hills, and out over the flats,
Many new sights and sounds are heard above the constant joyful noise of clack-clack-clack.
Now together arriving at the scheduled destination, the locomotive is unpacked.

Sometimes the locomotive would plan long journeys oftentimes in need of a nap.
When two special boxcars connected to the front line, of excitement there is no lack.
With more luggage and space needed, this locomotive needs to add some racks.

Occasionally before making plans perhaps out in front it should toss a hat.
Surprisingly at a crossing the joined locomotive seems to have become out of whack.
Billowing smoke begins to roll up to the sky from that locomotive stack.

Those formed clouds are filled and painted with many shades of the color black.
The locomotive has begun to show signs of wear and widening cracks.
This heavy overload of freight makes managing sharp curves seem like a boxing match.

Disconnected and alone, the locomotive has a schedule planned for a jumping jack.
On top of this high incline filled with dreams and wonders I have my overflowing sack.
This locomotive on new rails merges stronger than ever as time has proven that.

Evil Ways

Those set guidelines you expect people around you to obey.
From the look on their faces they appear to be dismayed.
You think they are blind to your evil ways.

Many facts you enjoy twisting and distorting in your own evil ways.
Through smiles to others so honestly the messages you try to convey.
Your mind's translation to you seems to make everything okay.

That outward façade is quite a convincing display overshadowing your evil ways.
To appear forgetful again that quest you so well display.
Selfishly you expect pity to come in abundance your way.

Things beneficial only to you are important in your evil ways.
Like all other times in greed you again have become carried away.
Manipulating others is the game you so well play.

Attract the attention of some to hurt the feelings of others you may.
Only you are the loser, as alone you will be sitting lost someday.
Like a clear glass of water, transparent to everyone are your evil ways.

The bag of old tricks you tightly grasp in your clutches clinging to your evil ways.
The sad sack is worn and tattered as the strings from overuse have become frayed.
Is all of your corruption really worth the price as your evil ways portray?

Time may heal some punctured wounds caused by your evil ways.
Those everlasting scars are constant reminders of where your deceptions preyed.
You struggle for the answers while in glory we walk without your evil ways.

Leftovers

Leftovers from yesterday's adventures today with you I share.
Long scattered thoughts are gathered in visions now at them I quietly stare.

Those leftovers lead me on this journey of remembering a life for which I cared.
These unending reminders will forever follow me everywhere.

Chances taken beyond reason bring smiles and laughter of your leftover antics dared.
Words of kindness filled the deepened gap once believed even time could not repair.

Hidden in the clouded wisdom I find this gift of leadership from leftovers you prepare.
This father conveyed unspoken words in eyes of glint of what only his child was aware.

Since your lights have darkened, my life is illuminated in your leftover's blinding glare.
Brightly shining is this path before me yet at times I felt life seemed to be so unfair.

These leftovers have become a precious treasure for me my mind declares.
From your hand to mine I grasp this wealth of strength with a love beyond compare.

Along the way from time to time these leftovers with others I may need to share.
Memories from a life so precious, this was one of a kind so unique and rare.

Mother's Flower Garden

Give her flower seeds to sow.
She planted them in a row.
Others she would toss and scatter to and fro.
Let it rain, sleet, or snow.
They would soon begin to grow.

She would weed, rake, and hoe.
Some grew tall while others trailed real low.
These to pick, those are for show.
They would dance and prance as the warm winds blow.
The shining sun made the petals glow.

Fill a vase with water, wrap it with a ribbon, then attach a bow.
Off to a friend or neighbor's house she would go
To give a bouquet from Mother's flower garden the seeds she sowed.
She has gone to Heaven now we know.
Love and kindness still blooms in Mother's flower garden here below.

Look Around

I walked into the room today to take a look around.
Everything is still in place but I don't hear a sound.
From room to room I swiftly went going upstairs and down.
Passing by the dresser mirror, on my glancing face I see a frown.
The front porch steps still attached where I used to lounge.

The old rosebush blooms behind me as I stand there to look around.
Underneath the pine and hemlock trees their needles cover the ground.
As I make my way to the garden perhaps someone will be found.
Years ago the hollow was filled with echoes from the barking coon hounds.
Scattered memories on loose pages of my mind into a book will be bound.

My mind is changing scenes staying unattached as I quickly look around.
You all came back for a moment now joyfully I am dancing like a clown.
Daydreams fill the gaps of loss while adventures waiting up ahead of me mound.
Back in reality here we are offered this glorious chance to go round and round.
I will come here and linger again, but now smiling I really must drive into town.

Little Lamb

In the heavenly clouds today I saw and heard a little lamb bleating.
The little lamb had tufts of wool above its eyes for characteristic markings.
Could it be the little lamb from the newspaper story sending Easter blessings?

The story read of the little lamb having needed bottle feedings.
Oh how farm animals can tug at one's heartstrings in just one meeting.
Caring, sharing, unconditional love they bring to young and old unending.

For this little lamb its mission on earth was not surviving.
No it has a far greater destination off the farm it was planning.
The story reads the farmer one night of the little lamb was dreaming.

He himself had become a shepherd once again and in Heaven he heard bleating.
The green lush fields he saw soon will be filled with Heaven scents of haymaking.
Beyond the grassy rolling hillside someday for all the little lamb will be waiting.

I hope, back on my sheep farm, homestead tears for me they are not shedding.
Now on this white cloud I close my big brown eyes, my little woolly head resting.
It is real fluffy and for me little lamb it has gilded golden edging.

Tomorrow, up the golden path, on the pink clover heads I will be nibbling
Then later bounce over to the fields of hay that look like threads of gold little lamb is bleating.
Across the brook lined with violets by the waterfall there are playmates for little lamb standing.

In the same newspaper story is a cookbook to purchase advertising.
This little lamb has a much higher IQ than you might expect; this is not surprising.
It has already escaped the thought of what any cook might have been surmising.

From the cookbook perhaps the lamb stew recipe is missing!
Put ham on the Easter table I can hear this little lamb bleating.
Annually perhaps that message would be worth the Little Lamb repeating.

If the sky above is filled with clouds making life seem dull and darkening,
Listen closely—sunnier days are ahead; you can hear the little lamb bleating.
That story of the little lamb bleating has now become this Easter greeting.

Butterfly Wings

Today at the post office I saw a small stuffed bear with attached butterfly wings.
It hung there for sale on display among the other things.
I purchased some stamps and also the bear; along home with me it I did bring.

Four little butterflies, appliqués on the bear's chest, ear, paw and foot they do cling.
This bear has a mission as through my mind this thought did ring.
With Easter approaching, there are many signs of spring.

I was told of a pastor who from an illness has been suffering.
To return emerged from a cocoon like a butterfly he wrote in the church bulletin.
This bear with butterfly wings I placed inside a gift box and tied it with a string.

Now this gift I gave to my mother-in-law to deliver to him.
For the pastor is this post-office bear with attached butterfly wings.
For certain, *what could be inside this gift box*, the pastor is now wondering.

Showers of get-well blessings through the air from everywhere will fling
When inside this box he spies the bear with attached butterfly wings.
Those angels are rejoicing in heaven as they hear his heart begin to sing.

Selectively these words are placed in the mind of a stranger for poetic composing.
With the butterflies' help, this pastor's wish fulfilled, his health steadily improving,
God will send strength and encouragement disguised sometimes in ways surprising.

Do not question why things are attached, such as a bear with butterfly wings.
Sometimes one's life could be compared to that of a ride high in the air on a swing.
This bear's mission is completed as to others repeated; we thank You, God, our King.

Holiday Tea

Today the ladies are stopping by the house for a holiday tea.
Time seems to have a way of escaping me.
I really could sip a cup of holiday tea.

I used to take a lot of time to sew.
This Christmas apron I made many years ago.
I wear it to serve this holiday tea, its strings tied into a pretty bow.

Lit are the candles on the table beside the candy dishes filled.
The train travels beneath the tree branches still.
Tea is steeping as the guests come inside to escape the winter's chill.

Today a poinsettia was brought to me.
Its color is cinnamon, I do believe.
That is quite a change from the usual red, indeed.

Now blown away are those autumn leaves.
The landscape is a display of Christmas deer, colored lights and many wreaths.
For now a cup of holiday tea would enhance this Christmas glee.

The grandchildren make the hustle of holiday shopping fun.
Then to attend so many holiday events I have just begun.
To have this holiday tea with the ladies this is a special one.

Many drifting snowflakes and howling winds bring the winter season.
Its magical beauty glistening on sloping hillsides is quite pleasing.
To take time to have a cup of holiday tea, I can always find a reason.

Kaleidoscope

For Christmas many years ago, we three sisters in magic had come to believe.
When from an aunt and uncle a gift of a kaleidoscope we did receive.
Those colors and shapes would all fall into place, as a design it did weave.
We anxiously wondered what on the next turn we would see.

This was a swell, fun gift for us three sisters, indeed.
For more elaborate entertainment there was no need.
The aunt and uncle and two sisters are now in Heaven as the gift remains with me.
Their loving faces in my mind, forever impressed, I will see.

Now there's time to spare, if only those memories we could share.
Its beauty is beyond compare,
As into the Kaleidoscope once again I do stare,
Relaxing here on my rocking chair.

I still recall when we received the gifts on that day.
Now here beside me that kaleidoscope stays.
If sometime in a toy store you might see one on display,
Perhaps a kaleidoscope you could buy to give away.

Give this beautiful gift to small children on Christmas Day.
Let them find the same joy as I did at play.
As they turn the kaleidoscope, slowly those designs it will display
While with me always, those happy, joyful memories will stay.

Candle in the Window

There is a chill through the solemn darkness this cold winter night.
Scattered stars up in the far-distant sky shine so bright.
Those blustery winds sting one's face with an icy bite.
There, a candle in the window is a welcome sight.
Was it placed for someone's way to light?

Did the candle in the window come from his childhood home?
Was it bought at an antique shop, its original owner unknown?
Can it provide a comfort to someone who lives alone?
Through the eyes of many a stranger, its light has shone.
Its beauty through the night casts a warming tone.

Does it illuminate a table where those kind folks dine?
Was it placed in remembrance as an unforgotten memory rewind?
Gaze into the light of the candle in the window for a time.
It will create its own purpose as through your eyes it shines.
The answers to these questions are in your mind to find.

The coming holiday season is so very near.
Those many Christmas bells ring in the air so clear.
Let the candle in the window on your pathway bring cheer.
Put its picture on a greeting card to send to someone dear.
Then it will become a lighted memory throughout the coming year.

Christmas Wreath

From the attic I brought the Christmas wreath once more.
The bow is missing that it once wore.
When I go shopping, I will purchase a new bow at the store.
Maybe it will be red, green or gold—so many choices to explore.

I will make this Christmas wreath more beautiful than ever before.
The real reason for this holiday season, I adore.
I could place a manger scene on the wreath and fasten it secure.
On the Christmas wreath some fake snowflakes I could pour.

Again this holiday, the Christmas wreath I will restore.
Its unending circle is filled with Christmas memories galore.
Each year, I hang it on the front door.
It always is a welcome sight; that is for sure.

I will not take this Christmas wreath to the attic anymore.
After Christmas I will deck it out in a Valentine décor;
In March, on it put shamrocks from the box on the attic floor;
Next, place on it a display of daffodils and Easter bunnies by the score.

With flags and red geraniums we can celebrate July 4th as rockets soar.
Now, I will cover it with shells I collected from the seashore.
Underneath it all, this Christmas wreath has a secret stored.
Those sunflowers are waiting patiently to make the autumn encore.

Halloween ghosts and witches bring to this Christmas wreath folklore.
Pumpkins, corn, and turkeys are now attached beside the dried apple cores.
This sure was fun, and none of the seasons was ignored.
Everlasting beauty shines through the changes this Christmas wreath endured.

Holiday Decorating

These December winds are brisk and cold as they blow.
That early morning frost looks like a newly fallen snow.
So much I need to do today and lots of places I must go.
This holiday decorating has my mind in a tizzy; see, it shows.

Many cookies, pastries, and candies must be made or bought.
Simplicity would be so easy, I thought.
Holiday decorating is so much fun; I almost forgot.
The tree with garland and lights are placed in just the right spot.

Years of collecting ornaments packed away—there are many, many.
Santa Clauses, snowmen, trains, bells, stars, angels, and candles are plenty.
Each year is a different holiday decorating theme; this year I haven't any.
One colorful splash connecting the years would glow like a new penny.

The days are shorter, but these holiday decorating ideas can be unending.
This new decorating twist clearly leaves thought for much amending.
Up on the mantel are angelic scenes with angels ascending.
The holy manger reminds us of the Christmas story descending.

Things are put away, and that space the poinsettias are lending.
I make a gift list and dinner menu closer to Christmas that is pending.
I love to address cards to friends—old and new—for early sending.
To enhance the outside holiday decorating, on snow I am depending.

Much time it takes to complete this holiday decorating season.
Hang stockings, for soon from the North Pole Santa will be leaving.
Colorful ribbon edged with wire makes creating fancy bows pleasing.
To try planning next year's theme now is neat, but that is beyond reasoning!

Tea Parties in Heaven

Let us visualize in our minds today
We are going to a place far away.

It is up above the clouds so blue.
Oh how can this be true?

Many unanswered questions as we go
As we ascend from here below,
So many friends' faces we will know,
Making our way drifting to and fro.

As we ascend the golden stairs
I wonder, will there be tables and chairs?
Through the pearly garden gate I will stare over there.

Look! On the rack, I see a large array of hats.
They are covered with flowers, ribbons, and this and that.

I have begun to wonder, can this all be?
On the tabletop, a teapot I see.

It is beside the basket
That is filled with packets.

Wrapped in golden packets is tea carefully placed for each of us to take
With words inscribed *Angelic, Calm, Serene, Peaceful,* and *Anticipate.*

Then there are blends of tea labeled
Home at Last, Here to Stay, Forevermore, Bless Me, and *Heaven's Heavenly.*
Now I must choose,
Which tea will it be?

So many more friends' faces I have begun to see.
They now have come and will join me.
Then as we begin to chat,
We pause in amazement as He sat on the chair
By the stairs of gold.
In His hand, a cup He holds.

"Let's have a tea party!" I heard someone say!
Oh, do you think He would mind if we stay?

This is your eternal home. Just as I have planned.
You all have just arrived in the Heaven Land, we are told.
We chose our hats, and our packets of tea we begin to unfold.
We place them in our cup. The cups seem to be made of the same mold.

Then, as we gather around Him, we stand.
We pick up our cup with our right hand.
We begin to sip upon His command.

All joining Him for this favor,
Each of us chose a different flavor
Prepared for us by our Lord and Savior.

Now, as we bow our heads and begin to pray,
We know this all will be real someday.
Lord, help us, as we journey along life's way,

For we know not when our time will be.
Till then, we will sit and sip our tea.

Together we will pray and visualize away the days,
And dream of when we would join Him again for tea—
Someday, someday, someday.

Together we will pray until that day—
Lord, yes, that day—
When we will all be coming home to stay.

The Poet

Inside me there lives the poet.
Many times I have come to know it.
Its face really never shows,
Sometimes moving fast and then so slow.
Through my mind it needs to go
As the lines in words, they do flow.

On a paper, with a pen, I write them down,
Sometimes changing them all around.
From the beginning until the end,
The poet's words I will defend.
Never knowing what it will send,
This is a blessed, trusting friend.

As through my mind it stops to say
Let's write another poem today.
Upon my face, it brings a smile
As I take the time to sit awhile.

Over the years, I have missed many lines
When I do not stop to take the time
To listen as you sent those words and rhymes.
I will write them down some other day,
As I get so caught up in life's busy ways.

Now I realize this is almost like a game.
Those lines never come back to me the same.
They pass through my mind, and then they are gone.
Then quietly, swiftly, they move on.

Here, upon life's path, I will walk.
Now and then, I will hear you talk.
Now, with those visual lines, I see
These many poems you have composed for me.

Your presence surrounds me in a deep and silent still.
The air, it sometimes brings a chill
Followed by a flash of lines
Filled with warmth brighter than sunshine.

Nevermore myself I need remind,
This gift, it travels through my mind.
Its face I cannot see from here inside me
I wonder, oh, how I wonder, who could the poet be?

Today, in a mirror, my eyes caught your stare.
Throughout life, I now realize you were always there.
For together we have gone everywhere.
Those many words in lines we shared.

Another of life's lessons learned,
I close this day without concern.
The poet inside me, it lives.
All of my thanks to God above I give.

I pray each day you take the time
To listen to those words and rhymes.
They are sent to me from Heaven above,
Filled with His everlasting love.

If, into that mirror, at that face, today you gaze,
Then turn away to give God praise.
With light in your eyes, you will always find a way
As you travel through life from day to day.

If you are wondering how all of this I know,
You see, the poet who lives inside
Just told me so!

CPSIA information can be obtained at www.ICGtesting.com
Printed in the USA
BVOW10s0509241215

430889BV00001B/1/P